Columbian Red Tail Boa as Pets

A Pet Care Guide for Columbian Red Tail Boas

Columbian Red-Tail Boa Anatomy, Purchasing, Care, Cost, Shedding, Housing, Health, Food, and More Included!

By: Lolly Brown

Copyrights and Trademarks

All rights reserved. No part of this book may be reproduced or transformed in any form or by any means, graphic, electronic, or mechanical, including photocopying, recording, taping, or by any information storage retrieval system, without the written permission of the author.

This publication is Copyright ©2019 NRB Publishing, an imprint. Nevada. All products, graphics, publications, software and services mentioned and recommended in this publication are protected by trademarks. In such instance, all trademarks & copyright belong to the respective owners. For information consult www.NRBpublishing.com

Disclaimer and Legal Notice

This product is not legal, medical, or accounting advice and should not be interpreted in that manner. You need to do your own due-diligence to determine if the content of this product is right for you. While every attempt has been made to verify the information shared in this publication, neither the author, neither publisher, nor the affiliates assume any responsibility for errors, omissions or contrary interpretation of the subject matter herein. Any perceived slights to any specific person(s) or organization(s) are purely unintentional.

We have no control over the nature, content and availability of the web sites listed in this book. The inclusion of any web site links does not necessarily imply a recommendation or endorse the views expressed within them. We take no responsibility for, and will not be liable for, the websites being temporarily unavailable or being removed from the internet.

The accuracy and completeness of information provided herein and opinions stated herein are not guaranteed or warranted to produce any particular results, and the advice and strategies, contained herein may not be suitable for every individual. Neither the author nor the publisher shall be liable for any loss incurred as a consequence of the use and application, directly or indirectly, of any information presented in this work. This publication is designed to provide information in regard to the subject matter covered.

Neither the author nor the publisher assume any responsibility for any errors or omissions, nor do they represent or warrant that the ideas, information, actions, plans, suggestions contained in this book is in all cases accurate. It is the reader's responsibility to find advice before putting anything written in this book into practice. The information in this book is not intended to serve as legal, medical, or accounting advice.

Foreword

If you're the kind of person who loves to be given tight hugs, well then, a boa constrictor snake species might be the suitable pet for you! You'll receive a wild hug from these wonderful species especially from the fave in the family – the Columbian Red Tail Boa!

The Columbian Red Tail Boa is one of the most widely kept boa species as pets. There are nine recognized sub – species of the boa family and the sub – species also vary in localities all over the world. The Columbian Red Tail boa is also known as the "red – tailed boa" or you can also refer to is as simply the "common boa" but Columbian Red Tail sounds cooler and exotic isn't it?

The true species of the red – tailed boa is the wild boa constrictor which ranges in countries like Brazil, Suriname, Peru and Guyana. They are much larger than the average domesticated Columbian red – tail boa. Some boa constrictors are also found in the South Eastern region of Colombia but it's rarely seen.

Columbian Red – Tail boas might be from a constrictor family but you will surely enjoy their company because their personality is docile and has no restrictions when it comes to having fun with you!

Table of Contents

Chapter One: Get to Know the Columbian Red – Tail Boa! .. 7

    The Boa Constrictor Imperator 8

Chapter Two: The Columbian Red – Tail's Anatomy 13

    Anatomy of a Boa Species 14

Chapter Three: Questions to Ponder Before Purchasing a Columbian Boa 23

    Frequently Asked Questions 24

Chapter Four: The Snake Starter Kit 35

    The Starter Kit 36

    Cage Size 43

Chapter Five: Regulating Lighting and Heat 47

    Temperature and Humidity Levels Guidelines 48

    Lighting Requirements 55

Chapter Six: Feeding Columbian Boa Constrictors 57

    Pre – Killed vs. Live Preys 64

    DIY Live Prey Killing 68

    Tips on How to Feed Frozen Prey Items 72

Chapter Seven: The Shedding Cycle 75

    The Shedding Cycle FAQs 76

Chapter Eight: Instant Solutions for Health Care Problems 83

    Regurgitation Syndrome 84

Lethargy	87
Respiratory Problems	88
Fecal/ Urine – Related Problems	90
Feeding Issues	92
Handling after Feeding	95
Chapter Nine: Breeding Boas	99
Pre – Conditioning	100
Sexual Maturity	101
General Care and Husbandry	103
Chapter Ten: Columbian Boa Constrictor Care Sheet	105
The Columbian Red – Tail Care Sheet	106
Glossary of Snake Terms	121
Photo Credits	129
References	131

Chapter One: Get to Know the Columbian Red – Tail Boa!

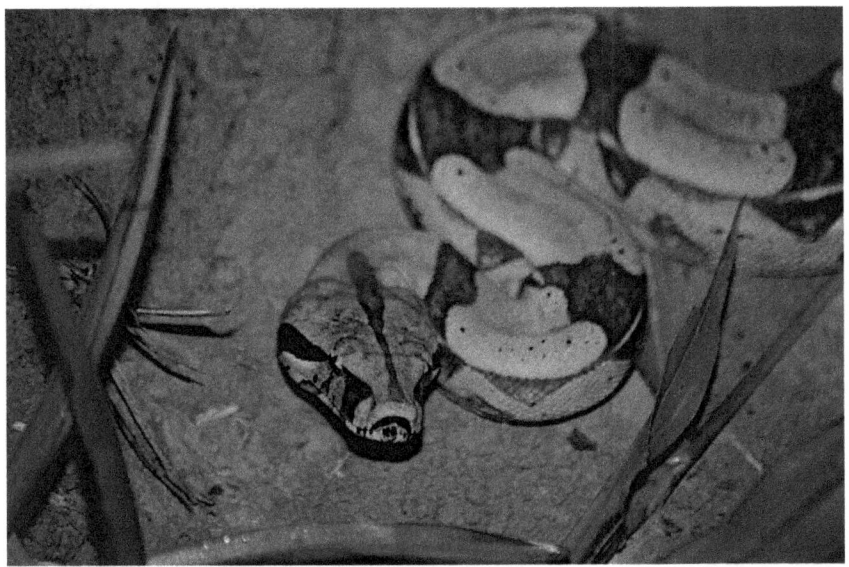

Columbian red – tails have become quite a popular pet in the reptile world because of its docile nature and soothing personality; their laid – back personality will surely make you feel "chill" all the time and they can also be a stress reliever after a long day of work. They might be docile but they're also inquisitive creatures just like their relatives in the boa family. In fact, the red – tail boas are more curious in their environment compared to other snake species. This chapter will show you what kind of world revolves around the lives of the Columbian Red – Tail species.

Chapter One: Get to Know the Columbian Red – Tail Boa
The Boa Constrictor Imperator

The Columbian Red – Tail boa originated in Columbia, and its main physical characteristic that differentiates it from other boa species is its reddish – brown colored markings or snake patterns on its tail. It's also a different variety of boa constrictor in the boa family. They inhabit semi – arid forests, rain forests, and also woodlands.

Just like other snake species, the Columbian red – tails are nocturnal, and they spend most of their day hiding among rocks, tree roots, and underground burrows. Due to their size, they aren't really considered as great tree climbers because small branches usually can't support their weight especially once they've reached a certain age. Some of the Columbian red – tails are also found swimming in the water as a way to cool themselves during humid days.

The common boa can reach up to about 10 feet while some can even get to 12 feet. Female species are relatively larger than males. They also has quite a long life span especially in captivity, they can live for around 30 years! Now that's a long time of constricted hugs right there!

Chapter One: Get to Know the Columbian Red – Tail Boa

Captive Columbian boas are quite adapted to human handling and they're very docile. Just a word of precaution though, they might be calm and friendly but you still need to keep in mind that they can still snap at any time so make sure you're prepared to get bitten; some snakes can also become aggressive without warning – consider this part of the job.

Speaking of bites, the Columbian red – tails are non – venomous snakes which means that you're quite safe despite of getting snapped on at times. In the wild, they initially bite their prey before quickly coiling around it and use their constricting/ squeezing powers to eventually squash their prey – it's a slow death for their prey. Boa species in general don't always hunt for their food, unlike most animals in the wild, that's just not their style! What they do is to do a camouflage and blend in with their environment to get near their prey or attack once they see a 'walking food' around. The Columbian red – tails including its relative species have heat sensing nerves on their lips that aids them in locating their prey. They usually feed on birds, lizards, mice, rabbits,

Chapter One: Get to Know the Columbian Red – Tail Boa

and other animals. In the wild, they only a few times in a month especially if they've eaten quite a huge prey.

Similar to other boa species, female Columbian red – tails lay around 15 to 40 baby snakes in just one clutch! The moms usually give tough love to their young because they don't protect their babies once they're born, and couldn't care less about their new eggs.

Nevertheless, in general they can tolerate humans handling and cuddling them. You'll notice how they will enjoy being in your arms, around your neck, or chilling in your shoulders. They will appreciate your body warmth, and will crawl all over you to show their love or just get some heat; after all they're cold – blooded animals!

If ever your pet boa has some kind of aggressive attitude, you may need to adjust your parenting style! It might be too constricting for these natural constrictors! Check the enclosure, the food they eat, the temperature levels and your overall husbandry because you might have done something they don't particularly like.

In general, the Columbian Red – Tail boa is a great household pet for reptile lovers of all levels! It's perfect for

Chapter One: Get to Know the Columbian Red – Tail Boa

first time snake keepers, or even snake hobbyists. The species remains to be a cornerstone in the reptile community, and due to its appealing patterns and colors they continue to attract more potential keepers.

The things you've learned in this chapter are just the tip of the iceberg! You'll learn more about this wonderful creature in the next few chapters including their anatomy, housing requirements, feeding guidelines, health concerns, breeding, and important husbandry tips! Welcome to the world of the boas!

Chapter One: Get to Know the Columbian Red – Tail Boa

Chapter Two: The Columbian Red – Tail's Anatomy

This chapter will focus on the anatomy of a Columbian Red – tail boa so that you can better understand its nature. Part of keeping these kinds of creatures is to know their physical capabilities because it'll come in handy whenever you're performing other keeping duties such as feeding, shedding, handling, and overall husbandry. You'll get to know how they use their body parts and the special features they have that can't be found in other snake species.

Chapter Two: Columbian Red – Tail's Anatomy

Anatomy of a Boa Species

Body

Columbian Red – Tail boas belong in the family of *Boidae* (consists of boa and python species). Boa constrictors are Ectothermic or cold – blooded animals, this means that snakes aren't capable of producing their own heat which is why your pet red – tail boa will try to grab some heat from its enclosure and from you! The heat that they'll acquire from humans or their environment will help them in digesting their food and also ensures good health. They gather heat from the sun, rocks, artificial heat sources (ceramic heat emitters, heat lights, or heat pads), and human handling.

Lungs

Columbian red – tails have 2 lungs; the left and the right. Both of their lungs remain functional compared to other snake species from another family that only retained one lung (usually the right side). Both lungs are functional for all species under the python and boa family.

Scales

Most boa snake species have smooth scales or skin. In fact, the scales are made out of hard folds of skin. The scales of your Columbian red – tail allows him/ her to get a grip on surfaces whenever they climb or crawl on something. One of the best features of a Columbian boa is its soft skin which is why they are not icky to handle unlike other snake species. It would feel like a soft leather in your skin. The scale patterns have a variety of colors, so pick the one you prefer.

Vertebrae

The vertebrae of a boa species comprises about hundreds of backbone, each of which has a pair that's attached to its ribs. Each of the backbone controls one ventral scale. The movement of your pet Columbian red – tail is done by using their ribs. Their vertebrae are very

Chapter Two: Columbian Red – Tail's Anatomy

extremely strong and agile which is why some of them can straighten their bodies in the air with no sweat.

Ventral Scales

The stomach of a common boa is known as the ventral side. The ventral side contains long skinny skins known as ventral scales.

Head

One of the most fascinating features of any snake species for this matter is their head. With boa species, the shape and color of their heads are quite interesting compared to other common snake species. The patterns are unique and it blends very well in the environment they live in. Some has strips on their head while some has other pattern that morphs into various coloring. Some keepers like them because of their addicting appeal especially the head patterns.

Chapter Two: Columbian Red – Tail's Anatomy

Eyes

The eyes of a common boa are usually matched to the color or pattern of their head. The stripe pattern might continue to their eyes. It's also important to note that boa species don't have any eyelids that can be closed. Their eyes are protected by an ocular scale or an eye cap that's clear in color. The ocular caps are usually shed during shedding period. This eye caps dilate in the presence or even in the absence of light. You might notice that their pupils can be slit or wide open depending on the amount of light.

Ears/ Hearing Organ

As you know, all snake species don't possess any external ears. In fact, most boas are completely deaf which means that they can't hear any sounds BUT they can sense vibrations, and pick up low frequencies through their inner ear. This is why; you shouldn't place your pet near vibrating objects or put things like refrigerators, stereo speakers, and

Chapter Two: Columbian Red – Tail's Anatomy

electric fans among others on or below their enclosure. A state of constant vibration will make your pet very stressful.

Mouth

Columbian red - tail boas is quite adapted to eating preys that are larger than the size of their mouth. The lower jaw of your pet is not connected to their skull unlike in other animal species or in humans. This means that they can freely open their lower jaw to eat their prey. The muscles and ligaments of their lower jaw allow it to expand and go back to normal. Using this ability, they can open their mouth that's enough to swallow animals that has larger heads than them. The larger the boa, the larger the ability to extend their lower jaw; it also allows them to do a ratchet motion in order to pull their prey inside their mouths.

Windpipe

The adaptive glottis or windpipe of Columbian boas allows the snake to eat prey items that are larger than their

Chapter Two: Columbian Red – Tail's Anatomy

heads. It also enables them to still breathe even if they're swallowing their prey items. They often use their glottis to warn their predators whenever they feel threatened. They do this by inhaling a large amount of air and exhaling it out so that the air will be forced out of their windpipe and create a hissing sound.

Teeth

Columbian red – tail boas have a small – sized teeth compared to other snake species. The quality of the teeth though makes up for the lack of its quantity as these teeth are extremely sharp and can pierce animal skin. They have 2 rows of teeth that are located in the top jaw, and 1 row of teeth on their lower jaw. The teeth are also slightly curved in order to hold the prey and easily pull it inside. A bite from your Columbian red – tail boa is very painful so be careful when handling them especially the adults.

Chapter Two: Columbian Red – Tail's Anatomy

Tongue

The infamous forked tongue of the boa family is one of their precious body parts because it's literally their eyes and ears especially in the wild. When a snake flicks its tongue that usually means that they are picking up particles which are them deposited on the roof of their mouths – also known Jacobson's organ. The Jacobson's organ is the place where particles are identified. A flick of their tongue can help them detect whether they are in danger, if there's a prey around, or if they are being courted by a potential mate. If your pet Columbian boa are flicking its tongue actively and rapidly, it's usually a sign that he/ she is healthy.

Cloaca

Their cloaca is their vent area and it is found in their tail. This is usually how you can determine what the sex is of your pet Columbian red – tail. This is also where your snake urinates and defecates. It's also the place where the babies

Chapter Two: Columbian Red – Tail's Anatomy

are delivered. If you look closely, you can also see the spurs in both sides of the cloaca.

Spurs

Columbian red – tail boas have remnants of a pelvic organ where the hind limbs probably used to be attached before they evolved into the kind of snake species we now know. These anal spurs are quite larger and more defined in males than female boas. They also use it during mating. Male boas have retained their control over their cloacal spurs and they use it during mating female snakes.

Tail

Even if the Columbian red – tail boa seems to be "all" tail, their tails are actually from the vent area to the tip. This is where the "Red Tail" came from. Compared to lizards, boa species can't lose their tails because they don't have regeneration capabilities. You'll notice that your pet boa will

Chapter Two: Columbian Red – Tail's Anatomy

wrap its tails around you or anything to ensure that they get a good grip and prevent them from slipping out.

Chapter Three: Questions to Ponder Before Purchasing a Columbian Boa

In this chapter, we will take a look at the various factors you need to consider before you make the decision to purchase a Columbian red – tail boa snake. Impulse buying is the most common mistake of first time snake keepers only to find out later on that they can't either commit in keeping one or they can't afford the requirements needed for the snake to live an adequate lifestyle. The Columbian red – tail is a cute species especially when it's still small but you need to be aware that they will eventually grow long and heavy.

Chapter Three: Questions to Ponder Before Purchasing

Boa snakes like the Columbian red – tail aren't the disposable type of pets which means you can't just give it to rescue centers. They also live a long life of about 20 to 30 years which is why you need to be truly committed because that's a long time to keep a household pet. Boa constrictors often find themselves in placement services or wild life rescue centers because the owners aren't aware of their sheer size and can't handle the adequate requirements. This chapter will bring up questions that will answer the important factors you need to consider before buying a boa.

Frequently Asked Questions

How large will my pet Columbian boa become?

The red – tail constrictor grows to around 7 to 8 feet, and they can live for around 25 to 30 years in captivity. The size will be tantamount to the amount of feeding. For instance, if you feed your pet less often, they may not grow over 5 feet. On the other hand, if you do "power feeding" your pet may reach to more than 8 feet and weigh over 80 pounds.

Chapter Three: Questions to Ponder Before Purchasing

What colors are available for Columbian boas?

Columbian red – tails are appealing to the reptile community and among snake hobbyists because they have various coloration and patterns. More new morphs are entering the market and will soon be quite affordable to every enthusiast. Generally though, a Columbian red – tail boa has a tan – colored body with dark brown saddles or blotches in their skin. Their tails are blood red in color to a more copper or rusty shade. The price is anywhere between $75 to $200 depending on size.

Some of the popular genetic colors available are Pastel, Arabesque, Motley, Ghost, Albino, Snow, Sunglow, Salmon, Jungle, and Anerythristic. Other morphs include Paradigm, Pearlscent, and Prodigy.

The tail of my Columbian boa is not red now, will it ever be?

Unfortunately not. Usually, the color of the tail at birth will determine the general color of their tail. However, boa constrictors usually show a nice shade of body and tail colors every time they shed especially while they're still young. Pink or orange highlights in the tail may also come out as they get older, but with few exceptions, this is because in general, the color of their tail gets a darker and darker as they age.

The new ways of selective snake breeding may get better and the color traits may result to a better coloring of the body but maybe not the tail.

Are Columbian Red – Tail boas aggressive or docile?

As previously mentioned, this snake species is quite popular because of its docile behavior especially if they're properly treated and cared for. Frequent handling especially at a young age will make them used to human touch; this in turn will make them docile their entire life and an even tempered pet snake.

Having said that, you still need to keep in mind that their behavior is usually tied up to the current state that they're in. For instance, if a Columbian boa is in a pre – shed state, or you just fed them, they usually don't want to be handled – and if you do, they may display a defensive stance. If your boa seems to be aggressive or too defensive,

Chapter Three: Questions to Ponder Before Purchasing

you may need to adjust some things, perhaps their enclosure doesn't fit them, or the temperature is wrong. The aggressive behavior can also be caused by feeding problems, mistreatment, or illness.

It's highly recommended that you buy a captive newborn Columbian boa instead of a juvenile or matured one so that you'll be the one to raise it and influence a docile temperament. You should also purchase it from a responsible or certified boa breeder to ensure that the baby is healthy and of quality.

Can I handle my Columbian boa?

Of course you can! But there's a proper way of doing it so that the animal will feel comfortable and will not be scared. Make sure to always support their long bodies with both hands, and avoid making quick movements whenever you're approaching your pet otherwise he/ she will think that you're a predator. Never handle it directly at their head because that's another 'predator move,' your pet might mistake it as aggression and might even bite you.

Chapter Three: Questions to Ponder Before Purchasing

Keep in mind that these boa constrictors sense heat, so what you need to do is to hold their tail and support their mid body; try to move them a little and get used to you so that they can sense that it's just their keeper and not a threat before getting them out of the enclosure. Avoid holding your Columbian red – tail where it restricts its movement so as not to feel uncomfortable. Make sure to use one of your hands to support the head area, and the other to support the rest of the body up to the tail. Some Columbian boas may feel frightened if they feel like they're falling or slipping out so make sure to support them and let them use your shoulders, neck, or hands as grip.

If ever your Columbian boa already grew over 6 feet, make sure to handle it with another person. If you want to keep your pet boa docile throughout its entire life, you need to handle him/ her at least 2 – 3 times per week.

How can I tell the difference between a defensive stance and a relaxed posture?

A relaxed or laid - back Columbian boa is when its entire body is coiled up. This is their normal posture, so to

Chapter Three: Questions to Ponder Before Purchasing

speak. On the other hand, the defensive posture is when their body and neck is in sort of a double "S" position, and their heads might be raised. If you see your pet in this stance, approach with caution – or do not try to handle it at the moment because it could pounce on you anytime. If your pet wants to be left alone, he/she will usually create a hissing sound. Do not approach when your pet does a hissing sound because this is their way of signaling you to back off otherwise they will strike you. Your pet could be in a defensive position if it has health issues or if it's completely opaque. Keep these things in mind so that you'll know what you need to do with your animal.

Can I keep more than one Columbian boa and house them in the same cage?

Before answering this question, it's important to note the different snake species should never be housed together. For instance, if you have a boa species, and a ball python, it's a bad idea to put them in one cage. Other than territoriality issues, the spread of possible disease is very risky. Some

Chapter Three: Questions to Ponder Before Purchasing

keepers believe that if you can't afford a second cage, you most likely can't afford to care for a second Columbian boa.

It's not about whether 2 snakes can or cannot exist in one cage because healthy boas can be raised together but it's usually when something happens that you need to separate them – and usually, something does happen that will require you to give them their own space. They can be kept together for a period of time within the day but they should still have their own cages especially during feeding times, shedding period, or if in case they get sick to prevent being attacked/contagious. If you're planning to breed a male and female, that's perhaps the only times that you can house 2 boas together; some keepers can handle housing their 2 boas in one cage but if you're just a newbie keeper it's best to buy them separate cages because at the end of the day, they're still animals and you can't monitor them 24/7.

In line with this question, here are some common issues that will require separate housing:

- **Feeding:** If you think you can feed both of your Columbian boas at the same time within in the same

Chapter Three: Questions to Ponder Before Purchasing

enclosure, well, get ready to see some blood! If you managed to keep them both in one enclosure, you should feed them on separate containers to prevent constricting one another as they will most likely fight each other for food even if you each gave them one. After all, they're still predators. Never try to feed them inside the same enclosure and don't also try to stop their fighting if ever they do because you don't know how strong they can be.

- **Diseases:** Well, this is a no brainer. Of course, expect that if one of your Columbian red – tail gets ill, the other one may acquire the disease as well so if you don't want to have 2 patients at the same time, better separate their enclosures.

- **Stress:** This is usually the overlooked factor. You see, if you put two snakes in one cage, there will most likely be competition – in everything. Territoriality and dominance issues are very common among animals. Both of your boas will feel that they need to compete in order to get the best basking spot or hiding spot etc. If they feel stressed out, their immune system will weaken which can result to them being sick.

- **Record Keeping:** It's already hard to track records of one snake species, what more if there's two? If you're not yet a seasoned boa keeper, keeping track of both your pets can be very difficult. You will end up dividing your attention and forget which one have already defecated or regurgitated. This won't be good for your boas health in the long run.

- **Breeding:** If you are interested in breeding your male and female Columbian boa, it's best that you should still separate them until the time that you're ready to actually breed them. This is because if they're already housed together ever since, they will most likely not end up producing any offspring. Separating them for extended periods is a great way to initiate the mating and breeding cycle.

Chapter Three: Questions to Ponder Before Purchasing

- **Quarantine:** Whenever you acquire a new boa species, you need to make sure that it's quarantined which means that the new boa should first be separated from your other snake species for a period of time (usually 60 to 90 days). This is to ensure that the newly acquired boa is free of any sickness or parasites that could be passed on to your other snake species

Will my Columbian boa strike me?

Well, anything is possible even for the most docile creatures. As mentioned earlier, you have to take note of their current status, your pet will usually show you signs if ever he/ she wants to be left alone so pay attention to their behavior to avoid any attacks or bites. If you always handle your pet, he/ she will not see you as a threat. You have to always take precaution in your approach, and don't approach like a predator. If you find that your boa is curled up in a corner and you approach it real quick, it will most likely be defensive and it can strike your hands or face – and

Chapter Three: Questions to Ponder Before Purchasing

that's not your pet's fault. I mean, if someone approaches you from behind in a rapid way, you'll most likely be defensive as well. It's just the same for these animals. The best way is to slowly approach from under them or within their level – NOT from above their heads! Whenever you're holding them, let them explore you so that it wouldn't be scared or feel threatened.

Are Columbian boas messy?

Yes, Columbian red – tail boas can be quite messy whenever they urinate or poop. They usually don't defecate a lot but when they do; it's surely a chore to clean up. Full size Columbian red – tail boas can poop just like a full grown dog. They also can deposit huge amounts of urates every now and then which are why you may need to clean their cage at least once or twice a week as this is part of proper husbandry and of course to keep your pet clean. Your pet will urinate and defecate through the cloaca found at the base of its tail.

Chapter Four: The Snake Starter Kit

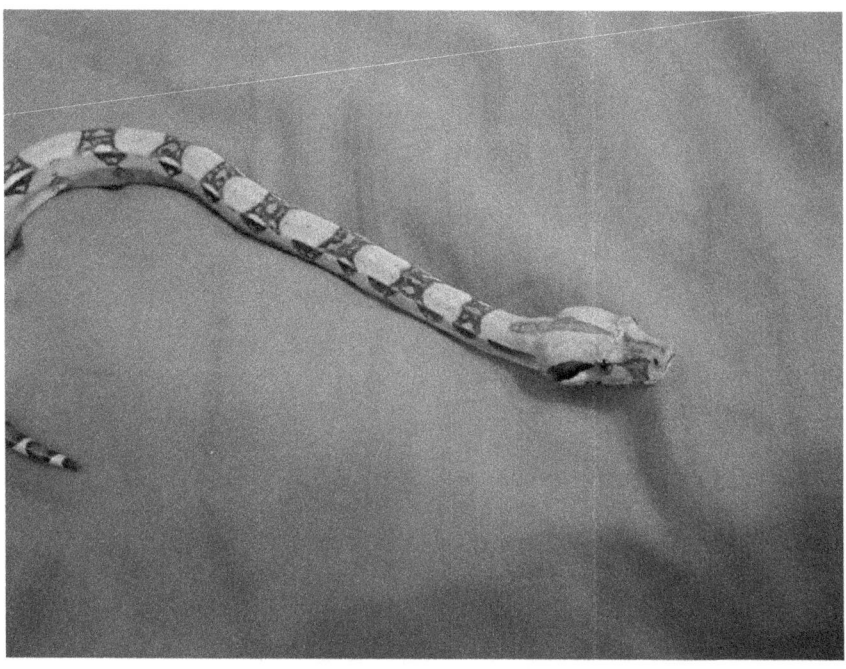

Every newbie snake keeper like yourself needs a "starter kit." A starter kit will include all the essential things you need for your pet boa. You'll get to know the materials used inside the enclosure including heat sources, cage furniture, thermometers and other measurement devices to help you initially set up a cage for your pet. The things that'll be mentioned in this chapter are the basic things and guidelines that you need to follow in order for your Columbian red – tail to be comfortable in its new home.

Chapter Four: The Snake Starter Kit

The Starter Kit

Custom Made Enclosures

Enclosures that are made out of plastic especially those that have built – in heaters are very durable for the lifetime of your Columbian boa. Custom made enclosures are great for keeping proper humidity and temperature levels plus it's also easier to clean compared to aquarium/ terrarium glass cages. It's very lightweight, can easily be heated, cleaned, transported and moved around your house which is why it's highly recommended for first time keepers.

Glass Enclosures

Another option is the aquarium – style glass enclosure. If you prefer this type of cage, make sure that you buy at least a 20 gallon tank size but if you can afford to purchase a much larger cage then it's much better so that you won't need to buy a larger one once your pet has outgrown the enclosure in just a few months' time. What most websites don't tell you is that glass enclosures are much more difficult to maintain temperature/ humidity

Chapter Four: The Snake Starter Kit

levels, and it's also much harder to clean. Generally speaking, glass enclosures are heavy and can be more expensive than plastic enclosures but if your goal is to also create an appealing display for your pet then maybe this is a better option.

Screen/ Top

Whether the cage you buy is made out of glass or plastic you have to make sure that it includes a screen top. Tightly secure it once you've set up everything including your snake because the last thing you want is for your pet boa to escape. Some will try to slide the lock open so always double check before leaving. Having a screen top adds to the struggle of maintaining the right temperature/ humidity levels since the warm air usually evaporates and comes out through the screener. You can cover half or all parts of the screen top with a cloth or cardboard to maintain proper levels.

Chapter Four: The Snake Starter Kit

Heater

You need to provide Under Tank Heaters (UTH) especially for glass enclosures. These heaters are usually attached to the bottom of the cage to provide your snake with their much needed warmth. If you bought a custom made/ plastic enclosures, you can opt to use Flex Watt Heat Tape instead of UTH. Belly heat is very important for your boa's digestion. Never use heat caves or heat rocks (more on this in the next chapter).

Clamp Heat Lamp

Some starter kit cages come with a clamp heat lamp or a built – in overhead lamp. If ever you use it as an additional heat source for your pet's basking area, it's highly recommended that you use a Ceramic Heat Emitter or CHE instead of using an incandescent bulb.

Ceramic Heat Emitter

CHE are heat emitters that don't have light source of any kind but it's the best option for constant heat source. This device can provide enough heat for basking and it can

Chapter Four: The Snake Starter Kit

also be used as ambient heat. It usually costs around $20 to 25 and it can last for a long time. The best part is that you don't need to turn it off unlike if you only use an incandescent bulb as your heat source (more on this in the next chapter). Ceramic heat emitters are available in 60, 100, 120, 150 wattages. It's best that you use a thermostat device so that you can control and regulate proper temperature.

Thermometer

Another important device is a thermometer. You'll need to buy 2 thermometers for your pet's cage. One is for the measurement of the basking area, and the other is for the ambient area. The thermometers should be installed inside the cage where you can easily see the temperature. You need to also buy a humidity gauge to help you control or regulate the humidity levels. It's also highly recommended that you purchase a digital thermometer because it's more accurate than the analog device. You can buy these at electronic stores.

Chapter Four: The Snake Starter Kit

Thermostat

Another MUST – HAVE device for starters is a thermostat. This is sort of your fail safe if in case your thermometers stop functioning. You need to protect and regulate your thermometers with a thermostat. You can buy various types of thermostat; some comes with dual devices, some has a nighttime drop feature that can automate cooling cycle and other features so it's up to your preference. These are usually accurate and a must have if you ever become interested in breeding your snake.

Water Dishes

Water dishes must be large enough for your pet to soak its entire body in. You'll notice that young Columbian boas will bathe quite often. There should be 2 water dishes placed inside the cage (if you have a large enclosure); the larger one should be on the ambient/ cooler area while the smaller dish should be in the basking area as this could help in humidity levels and also be used for drinking; having 2 bowls will also prevent your pet from compromising the level of heat required whenever they need water. You can

Chapter Four: The Snake Starter Kit

buy crock style bowls or ceramic types that are thick and heavy so that your snake won't be able to turn it upside down.

Clean Water

What would water dishes be without fresh and clean water? Make sure to check the water every day because your snake will most likely defecate in it. If you notice that your pet constantly soaks itself in water or he/ she bathe much often than normal then your pet may have a health problem; check it for mites or adjust the temperature because your pet might feel too hot.

Substrate

There are various types of substrate that you can use including cypress shavings, aspen, coconut bark or even plain newspaper (though newspaper is not highly recommended). Choosing a substrate is subjective because it will depend on what works for you and your Columbian red – tail. Shredded aspen is the substrate that's commonly used by keepers and breeders.

Chapter Four: The Snake Starter Kit

Branches/ Hiding Spots

Your pet will use branches as exercise opportunities, and they'll use hiding spots if they want to have some "me" time. Providing them with hiding spots creates a sense of security for them especially if the enclosure is quite large. Boas rarely climb so most constrictors may not use branches that much. You can purchase grapevine or similar products for branches, and choose from various synthetic caves as hiding spots. Make sure that it's suitable for the size of your boa because if the hiding spot is too big for them they might get stressed out.

You can also create a custom made hide box especially for baby/ juvenile boas. You can use ordinary materials found in your house like shoe boxes or Tupperware – style containers, cardboard boxes etc.

You can also purchase heavy type of hide boxes because this can be also beneficial whenever your pet is shedding. Some of them will rub their skin on the hide boxes during shedding period. Another popular form of hide box you can use is a shelf unit. This can also provide security for your boa snake.

Chapter Four: The Snake Starter Kit

Cage Size

For Baby/ Juvenile Columbian boas

The minimum cage size for a young or juvenile Columbian red – tail is 20 gallon glass tank (if an aquarium – style tank is what you prefer); or a 2'X2'X1 size for custom made cages or plastic enclosures. You shouldn't buy a 10 gallon sized cage for your boa even if they're just babies because it'll be inappropriate for them as they will easily outgrow it.

As previously mentioned, it's much better if you can afford to buy a larger enclosure for your pet at the onset even if they're still quite small in size. A large cage is beneficial not just for your pet's growing size but also because you'll have ample space to install the basic cage furniture like water bowls, branches, hiding spots, and substrate as well as external heaters like overhead lamps, thermometers, heat pads/ Under – Tank – Heaters etc.

Chapter Four: The Snake Starter Kit

If ever you can't afford to buy an adult – size cage yet, you can initially settle with the size aforementioned for your pet. Check out the diagram below for measurements:

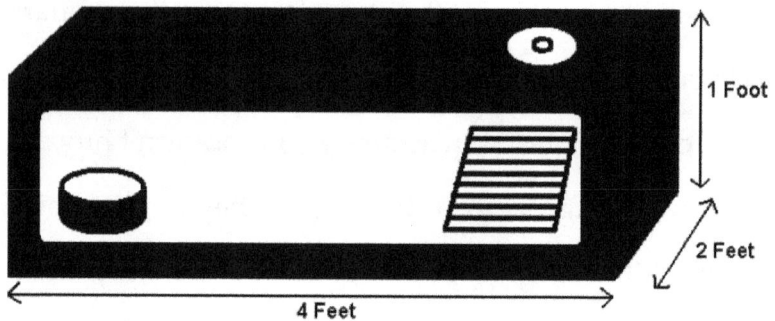

For Adult Columbian boas

If you will buy an adult – size Columbian boa then you need to buy a premium enclosure because space is what your adult boa will need. The general rule is that the cage should be at least ¾ as long as the snake's body, and the width should be a third of your boa's length. Custom made enclosures and glass tanks come in large sizes, and most of the cages are also durable and has safety lock features to secure your pet inside. Some custom made cages have features that provide regulating heat/ humidity levels but it

Chapter Five: Regulating Lighting and Heat

could be pricier. A 6' x 2' x 2' cage size is perfect for your adult pet's lifetime.

If ever you're planning in building custom made cages, just make sure to avoid unfinished porous/ wood surfaces as it'll be harder to clean and humidity/ water will definitely damage the material. The measurement is still the same 4' Wide x 2' Deep x 1' Tall to accommodate full – grown Columbian boas. Check out the photo below:

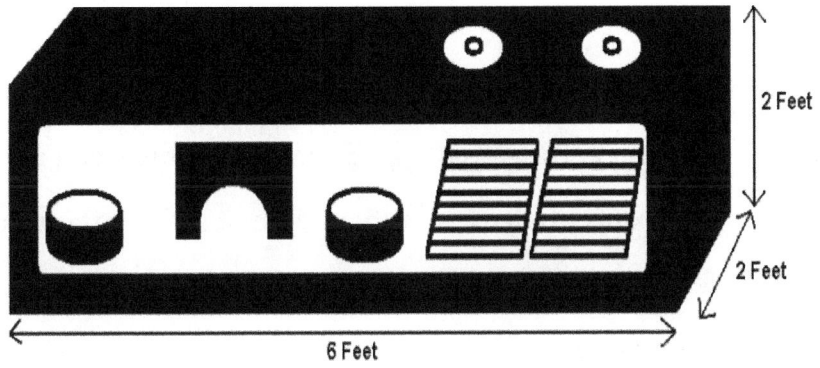

What should I use to disinfect/ clean my pet's enclosure?

Most keepers use a solution of Chlorhexidine with water, just go to the store and find the product of your choice. You must first remove your pet and place it in another container so that you can properly spot – clean the

Chapter Five: Regulating Lighting and Heat

cage. Wipe the entire enclosure with the Chlorhexidine solution at least once or twice a month.

You can also use ONLY 10% of bleach and water solution and do so with caution. Make sure to rinse the entire cage thoroughly with clean water in order to remove any bleach/ chemical residue. Completely dry the enclosure off before returning all the cage furniture and your pet snake inside.

You can also ask your vet if he/ she is selling a Chlorhexidine solution since this is the same type of disinfectant that they use. A gallon will usually last for a year or so depending on usage. Even if you only clean the entire cage once/ twice a month, you must still do a routine spot cleaning at least every week, and change the water supply every day.

Chapter Five: Regulating Lighting and Heat

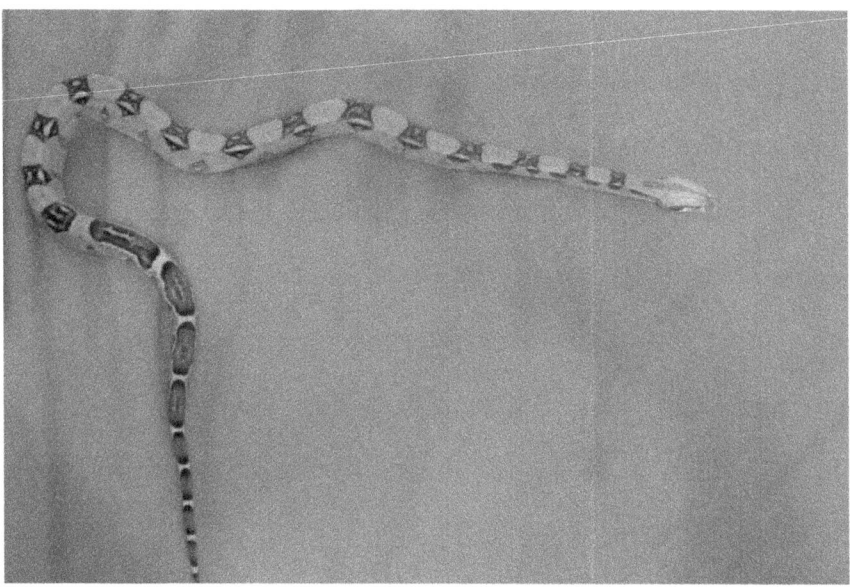

Providing the right size of enclosure and placing the cage requirements are all important but without the proper temperature and right humidity levels, your pet boa will most likely have some health issues. This chapter will serve as your guide when it comes to setting up the right temperature/ humidity levels as well as provide you with lighting options so that you can properly regulate the heat source/s of your snake inside the enclosure. Proper lighting and temperature will make your pet digest their food and also properly shed.

Chapter Five: Regulating Lighting and Heat

Temperature and Humidity Levels Guidelines

What is the right temperature level for my Columbian boa's enclosure?

Since Columbian boa constrictors are tropical species that means that their environment inside the enclosure should be maintained within a range of around 80 to 92 degrees Fahrenheit as this is somewhat the temperature they have in the wild. You should also provide a basking area with temperature levels that's below 90 degrees. The basking area will allow your pet Columbian boa to thermoregulate and also control its own body temperature. It's important that your boa constrictor has a place where it can warm up and also cool down. You should pick one side of the cage as the "basking area" – that's where you will need to place an overhead heat source and also a UTH heater that MUST be located on the same side of the enclosure. The other side will serve as the "ambient area" – this is the cooler part of the enclosure since it's away from the heat source.

Chapter Five: Regulating Lighting and Heat

Check out the photo shown below:

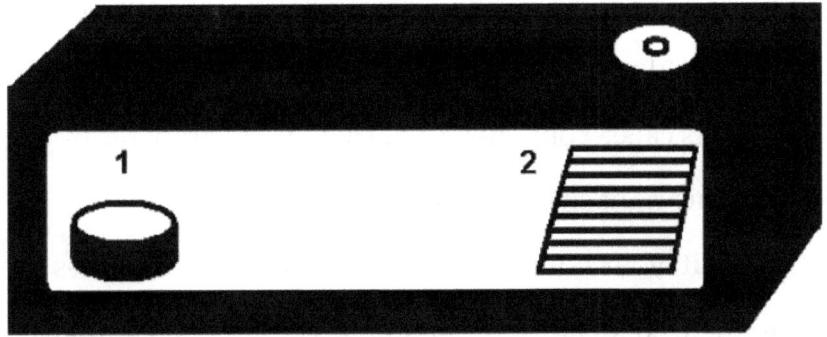

Ambient Area (1): Considered as the temperature of the air. This is the cooler side that's away from the heat sources. The temperature inside the enclosure on this area should be around 82 degrees Fahrenheit.

Basking Area (2): This is the side where the heat sources are located. The temperature should be around 90 to 92 degrees Fahrenheit. You can measure the temperature on or under the physical heating materials using a temperature gauge so that you can obtain the reading and see if it's enough to warm your pet boa.

Chapter Five: Regulating Lighting and Heat

Unless you are trying to breed your pet Columbian boa/s, the temperature measurement aforementioned should be maintained all year round. Your goal is that your pet snake should not feel too cold or too hot whenever you take it out of its cage. Your snake's normal body temperature if you do this right should be around 83 to 84 degrees Fahrenheit; your body temperature is around 98 degrees Fahrenheit, so ideally once you hold your pet, it should be just a bit colder than your own body temperature - and not hotter otherwise you may need to adjust the temperature levels inside your boa's enclosure. Proper temperature levels should be strictly followed and regulated because it greatly contributes to your pet's health. Most health issues that's linked with Columbian boas are temperature – related so make sure to get this right if you want your snake to live a healthy and long life.

What is the right humidity levels for my Columbian boa's enclosure?

In addition to temperature levels, another critical part of proper husbandry is the right humidity levels. You must

Chapter Five: Regulating Lighting and Heat

maintain a humidity level of around 50 to 60% at all times. It's important to note that the humidity levels are actually determined by geography or your location. In states like Florida or Texas, humidity levels can easily reach 60% compared to California which is just around 50% so make sure to adjust accordingly depending on your area of residence as it will highly affect the level inside the enclosure. Humidity level is very important to your pet's overall health because it helps them to properly shed their skin and digest their food. If you notice your pet boa has incomplete sheds or he/she is constantly soaking in water then these could be signs of improper humidity levels. These boa species is native to the tropical temperatures of Central America which is why you need to know the right levels that would allow your pet to thrive.

Keep in mind though that the temperatures given here are just guidelines, and the ranges we specified may or may not work out for your pet boa. There are some keepers who struggle to reach 50% humidity level while some can't maintain 60% levels mainly due to their locations, so make

Chapter Five: Regulating Lighting and Heat

sure to properly regulate their temperatures/ humidity levels because unlike in the wild, your captive snakes can't move from one place to another since they're just in an enclosure. You may need to use other materials that can create a humid environment such as misters, wet towels, substrate, plants, etc. which we will further discuss in the next section.

Tips on how to increase humidity levels:

- **Mist your pet boa periodically.** What you can do is to place a hot water in a spray or misting bottle and carefully mist it to your snake. The hot water will become quite warm once it's already sprayed so you don't need to worry about hurting your snake's skin though if you want to be sure you can test it first in your arms. Misting your pet or its enclosure can help raise humidity levels, and it will also benefit your Columbian boa during shedding period. Spraying cold water must be avoided because it will sort of shock your pet boa.

Chapter Five: Regulating Lighting and Heat

- **Place another water dish that's closer to the heat source/s.** Doing this will add to the evaporation process inside the enclosure and make it more humid. You must also provide another water dish on the ambient zone of the cage.

- **Cover all or parts of the top of the cage.** If ever you choose to use an aquarium style glass enclosure, it could be difficult to maintain humidity levels since there's a screen on top of these kinds of cages. What you can do is to cover at least ½ of the screen top using a piece of cardboard with pencil size holes poked in it. This can help raise and maintain temperature/ humidity levels.

- **Put a wet/ moist towel inside the enclosure.** You can try placing a wet towel or products similar to HumiMats inside the cage as this can absorb water and evaporates it over a period of 2 weeks.

Chapter Five: Regulating Lighting and Heat

Will it provide enough heat if I just use a heat lamp with a regular light bulb?

Well, the only way to know if this could work is to use thermometers and measure the temperature on both the ambient and basking zones of the enclosure. However, the danger of using a light bulb as your ONLY heat source is that it needs to be remained on for 24/7 in order for it to provide heat which means that you can't turn it off at night. Columbian boas will need 12 hours of light and 12 hours of dark so an incandescent bulb may stress out your pet since it will provide a constant light just to heat up the enclosure. It's better to also buy an Under Tank Heater (UTH) or ceramic heater emitters so that even if you turn off the light bulb at night time, your pet will still be provided with heat underneath the cage without direct light.

Can I use heat rock devices inside the cage?

NO! Never! If you do, your pet snake will get burned especially your baby boas since they won't know when to get off. These kinds of devices including heat caves will

Chapter Five: Regulating Lighting and Heat

provide a hot spot that's hotter than the basking area; make sure to keep all heat sources outside the enclosure.

Lighting Requirements

If the location of your boa's enclosure is close to the window where it can get enough sunlight during the day then you may not need to buy any overhead light source like light bulbs, but if it's not near any windows, you may need to buy an incandescent bulb or florescent lamps for daytime display purposes. Make sure to turn off the light at night to avoid stressing out your boa. Below are the lighting options for your pet's cage:

- **Incandescent Bulb:** These bulbs are a good source of adequate light and also heat inside the enclosure. Make sure though that it's placed above the cage where your boa can never reach it otherwise your pet will get its skin burned. Turn it off at night and don't make this your only source of heat. You can purchase

Chapter Five: Regulating Lighting and Heat

heat lamps and other varieties that are used for reptiles.

- **Florescent:** These lamps are the most widely used light source for snake species since the slender length usually fits most enclosures or aquarium styled cages. These bulbs also provide the best display light if you want to show your pet boa in all of its glory.

- **Full – Spectrum Lighting:** Repti Sun's full – spectrum lighting is not really required but if you want your pet to receive amounts of UVB and UVA wavelengths similar to what the sun produces, you can try it for your pet. Some keepers say it helps the food to be digested with UVB lights.

Chapter Six: Feeding Columbian Boa Constrictors

Feeding your pet boa the right prey items will go a long way because it will contribute to a healthy and longer life span. However, you need to know how to offer food items to them. Feeding reptiles like snake species is not as simple as you may think! You need to know feeding guidelines and you need to follow the tips you'll learn in this chapter to ensure that you're feeding your pet in a proper way. You'll get to know what, when, how, and why you

Chapter Six: Feeding Columbian Boa Constrictors

should feed your boa with the prey items listed in this chapter.

What should I feed my Columbian boa?

While most keepers believe that the best food source for most snake species is rats, the following prey items are also good food sources for your pet Columbian red – tail:

- Mice
- Hamsters
- Guinea Pigs
- Pinkie rats
- Gerbils

The rule of thumb is to offer smaller prey items for your Columbian red – tail newborns; it's best that you feed them weaned or 'pinkie' mice/ rats before you gradually feed them larger prey items as your pet grows. If you feed prey items that are too large for the current size of your boa, your pet will most likely regurgitate the food. Constant regurgitation can lead to various health issues including Regurgitation Syndrome.

Chapter Six: Feeding Columbian Boa Constrictors

Once your Columbian boa reaches its full – grown size, it's best that you start feeding them rabbits, jumbo rats etc. Some boas need to be fed with a couple of these large preys before they get satisfied which is why some keepers just settle with feeding their pet one large rabbit. You can order frozen bunnies, and they can also be thawed just like rats.

We highly recommend that you feed your pet boa with freshly thawed/ killed prey items instead of feeding them live rats or rabbits in order to prevent your snake from being injured during the 'food chase.' Your pet could be bitten by rats or rabbits during the food chase since these animals will do everything they can to survive their predator plus you're also exposing your pet to various types of parasites or diseases from these live preys. We will further discuss the pros and cons of feeding live preys versus pre – killed/ thawed preys.

How often should I feed my Columbian boa?

What I will recommend is to offer one prey item per feeding. Following the guideline given below will ensure that your pet will live a healthy and long life. Contrary to

Chapter Six: Feeding Columbian Boa Constrictors

other keepers, I think it's best that you should never do "power – feeding," – this is the process where you place another 1 or 2 prey items inside your pet's mouth as it swallows the previous prey. Power feeding is similar to forceful feeding, and some keepers do this if they want to rapidly grow their Columbian boas to great lengths in just a few months' time. Some keepers successfully use this method to grow their boas to their desired size, and some have also bred female species at 18 months of age using power feeding. However, it's almost without exception that such snakes live a shorter life span. You will notice that power – fed boas have abnormal size heads, and it's usually smaller and not proportionate to their body size. Feeding your pet properly and healthily will make him/her live for more than 20 years plus less trips to the vet.

Follow the recommended guidelines below or better yet ask your vet if these measurements are suitable for your pet:

Chapter Six: Feeding Columbian Boa Constrictors

Baby Columbian Red – Tail Boas (18 to 22 inches)

- This is suited for newborn boas up to 3 months of age. They should be fed with fuzzy or pinkie mice/ rats.

- You can feed them 1 prey item at least every 4 to 5 days.

- Sometimes if you feed pinkie rats/ mice, it will allow you to feed every 7 days which could be a much easier schedule for you. You can feed every Saturday if that's your choice.

Juvenile Columbian Red – Tail Boas (2 to 3 feet)

- This is suited for juvenile boas from 3 to 12 months of age. They should be fed with fuzzy or weanling mice/ rats.

- You can feed them 1 prey item once a week.

- In other places, weanlings are referred to as Rat Pups.

Chapter Six: Feeding Columbian Boa Constrictors

Yearling Columbian Red – Tail Boas (3 to 4 feet)

- This is suited for year - old boas from 1 to 2 years of age. They should be fed with small to medium size rats.
- You can feed your boa with 1 prey item or more (depending on the size of the rat/ desired growth rate) every 2 weeks to once a month.

Adult Columbian Red – Tail Boas (4 feet and up)

- This is suited for fully matured boas from 2 years of age and older. They should be fed with large to jumbo sized rats.

- The quantity or size of the rat you will offer to your adult boa will depend on their current girth and length.

- Adult female boa constrictors can be fed every 2 weeks while the male boas can be fed once a month. This will keep your pet compatibly sized especially if you plan on breeding them.

Chapter Six: Feeding Columbian Boa Constrictors

- You can also feed your adult boa with rabbits, but the size of the rabbit will depend on the current size of your adult Columbian boa.

If you follow the feeding guidelines aforementioned which are just 1 prey item at a time, you can expect your pet Columbian boa to grow to an average size of 7 to 8 feet. If you change your feeding guidelines, you will definitely change the growth rate of your pet. Before you change your pet's diet, make sure to consult it first to your vet. If you really need to change the diet, you may need to gradually do it and check first if it works out for your pet.

I also recommend placing the frozen/ thawed prey items inside your pet's enclosure, and just leave it there overnight. If you find that it's uneaten the next day, make sure to dispose the food, and just feed another fresh item.

It's also important to note that you should never handle the prey items as you place it inside your pet's cage because your hand can be mistaken as food! It's better if you use tongs or similar items to protect yourself. You shouldn't also handle your pet after preparing food items because your

Chapter Six: Feeding Columbian Boa Constrictors

hands will smell like rats/ rodents, and if your boa smelled that, he/ she can take a bite on you.

If your Columbian boa is a finicky eater, you can try feeding them live prey items, but I highly recommend that live preys should be your last resort. If your pet really prefers live food than thawed preys, make sure to monitor your pet after placing the live animal inside its cage to avoid any injuries to your snake.

Most snake species will eat at night, and they also prefer a varied diet so it's best that you offer various types of rodents/ rat species as long as it's free of diseases.

Pre – Killed vs. Live Preys

Almost every pet store, snake care guide books, and casual snake keepers will tell you that these species will only eat live prey items. I beg to differ. Columbian boas are one of the easiest snake species to convert into pre – killed or frozen prey items. Newborn boas can readily accept pinkie rats which mean that they're fine being fed with thawed/ pre – killed preys.

Chapter Six: Feeding Columbian Boa Constrictors

Captive bred and captive born snake species are already very far from their natural environment in the wild since they're considered as domesticated animals. You see, we are their food source which is why as responsible snake keepers, we should always provide what's best for them. Tossing a live rat inside the enclosure may have that 'predator feels' but this practice will eventually wound your pet boa or pass diseases to them. If you search online, you'll see the damages that are caused by live preys like rats to various types of snakes. Don't expect the rats/ rodents to not fight back; they may lose at the end but your snake will accumulate wounds in the long run and that'll be the source of their defeat.

Why Should I Convert My Boa to Eating Pre – Killed Preys?

Check out the reasons below:

- **Pre – killed prey items will make the offering/ removing of food easier.** The dead rodent can easily be placed inside the cage without you risking yourself

Chapter Six: Feeding Columbian Boa Constrictors

of it getting away. You can leave it during the day or even overnight without endangering your pet snake. You can also remove it safely the next morning if it's not eaten within the night.

- **Pre – killed prey items will make your snake less aggressive and friendlier.** If you create a habit of only offering pre – killed diet to your pet, then over time he/she will be more docile because your pet will recognize that the prey will be handed to them, and all they really need to do is to eat. No chase, no thrill, no striking of any kind (although some still do) and no 'predator feels.' It may sound boring but it's safe for your pet. You will see that over time, your pet will slowly approach the prey, and eat it without any struggle. They will take their time with their food without the risk of being bitten or stressed out unlike feeding live preys where they'll need to play as the hunter all the time – they're not in a jungle, they're in your house! Feeding pre – killed diet will eventually

Chapter Six: Feeding Columbian Boa Constrictors

turn your boa into docile and friendly pets because violence will not be in their 'vocabulary.'

- **Pre – killed diet will ensure that your snake will be hungry whenever it's feeding time.** Most boa constrictors will not eat if they're not hungry. Expect to see your pet to sometimes refuse the food you offer them. If you feed live prey and they don't feel like eating, they will have no choice but to kill and eat the animal anyway, and this could have effects on their health.

- **You won't need to see poor mice/ rats be killed by your pet.** Some owners especially newbies cringe at the sight of their snake constricting and killing the live rodents which is why it's easier for them to just feed pre – killed food items. It will also minimize the suffering of the rodents.

Chapter Six: Feeding Columbian Boa Constrictors

DIY Live Prey Killing

Another alternative way of offering a live prey without the 'thrill of the kill' is to pre – kill the rodents yourself, and offer it to your pet while the rodent is still warm. This is of course not for the faint of heart! Here's how you can do it:

- Grab the rodent by its tail. Quickly swing it back and forth, and then strike its small head on a hard floor or surface.

- Once it's killed, you can immediately feed it to your snake while it's still warm.

Another way is to use a Carbon – dioxide gas tank. You just need to place the rodents inside an enclosure and trap them with the carbon – dioxide air so that they can become unconscious and killed right away. You can search online on how you can create your own CO_2 enclosure. You may also try using a dry ice, and place it inside a Styrofoam box where the rodents are placed; this method is particularly

Chapter Six: Feeding Columbian Boa Constrictors

for those who are looking to raise their own set of rodents, and those who need to freeze the prey item.

How Can I Convert My Pet from a Live Prey eater to a Pre – Killed Prey feeder?

If your Columbian boas are in good shape, you should feed only pre – killed prey items for several weeks, at different times of the day and at night. Keep in mind that it won't hurt a boa constrictor to miss a meal every once in a while, they'll still survive. Some keepers give in easily and go back to feeding their pet but remember that this will not help you in converting your pet snake. So just nudge the feeling because they can survive and still be healthy even if they miss a meal. Check out the tips below:

- **Try feeding different sizes/ colors of rodents.** Some boas can be easily converted by offering different variety of rodents. Make sure that the prey item is warm; what you can do before offering it to your pet is to soak the rodent in warm water.

Chapter Six: Feeding Columbian Boa Constrictors

- **Use long tongs to hold the pre – killed prey item, and shake it in front of your snake.** Sometimes it's as simple as this to get your boa to be converted.

- **Use the hide box.** Some keepers will wait until their pet is inside of the hiding spots/ box before taunting the food to them. After a while, they'll use the tongs and attach the prey into it before taunting their snake. Oftentimes, the smell of the dead prey will entice the snake to come out and eat the food.

- **Leave the thawed/ frozen rodent overnight.** If your boa is a finicky eater, he/ she will prefer to just eat at their own desired time despite of being aware of the food inside their enclosure. What you can do is to just leave the prey item in the enclosure before you go to bed. Most boa species love to eat at night once the lights are out since they're nocturnal animals.

Chapter Six: Feeding Columbian Boa Constrictors

- **Feed small – sized live preys with a follow – up of pre – killed preys.** This method usually works for many snakes. Once you've fed a humanely killed prey to your pet, you can immediately offer thawed/ frozen preys. After doing this for a while, you can slowly start over this time with offering pre – killed items only.

Why Should I Convert My Boa to Eating Frozen Thawed Preys?

The next step is to convert your boa from eating pre – killed preys to frozen or thawed prey items. These rodents are usually vacuum packed, frozen from storage, placed in sealed containers, and fully thawed come feeding time. Check out the reasons of why you should eventually convert your pet to eating frozen thawed preys:

- Freezing the rodents will automatically kill any internal/ external parasite that the rodents may have.

Chapter Six: Feeding Columbian Boa Constrictors

- It's readily available and can be bought from various sources. You just need to defrost it for an hour before feeding it to your snake.

- Vacuum sealed containers allow long storage of prey items for 6 months to even 1 year.

- It's much cheaper than buying live prey items especially at pet stores. It can easily be shipped to your home for just a small fee.

Tips on How to Feed Frozen Prey Items

You must defrost the prey item, and NEVER attempt to feed your boa snake with a totally frozen prey. You need to thaw it and warm the prey item to the room temperature before placing it inside the enclosure.

Chapter Six: Feeding Columbian Boa Constrictors

You can use Rubbermaid containers that are big enough to hold a number of prey items. Check out the thawing tips below:

- Fill the container with cold tap water. Place the prey items inside and just let it stand for 1 hour. If you will thaw just a couple of rodents, you can do so for less than an hour.

- Never thaw the rodents as fast as you can because if you do, the mice/ rats could burst open once your snake bite into it due to improper thawing.

- After 1 hour, replace the cold water with lukewarm water and let it stand for around 15 mins.

- After 15 minutes, you can replace the lukewarm water with hot water prior to feeding so that the rodents will be warm to a feeding temperature as if they're just freshly killed. Warmed up rodents will exhibit an enticing smell for your pet boa.

Chapter Six: Feeding Columbian Boa Constrictors

- After running hot water, the next step is to drip dry them not towel dry.

- Once it's done, you can now feed the rodents using your tongs NOT your hands.

- These tips also apply if you need to thaw rabbits, you may just need to thaw it for more than an hour since they are bigger than rodents.

Chapter Seven: The Shedding Cycle

Your Columbian Red – Tail boa will undergo the so – called "shedding period" or cycle. Shedding period or shedding cycle in snake species are also known as Ecdysis. This is when your pet snake shed off their old skin so that it can be replaced with a new one. It is also a growth process for them. Whenever your snake is shedding that could also mean that they are growing longer. Proper husbandry particularly setting up the right temperature and humidity levels will make the shedding process easier for your pet.

Chapter Seven: The Shedding Cycle

Some snake species have a hard time shedding because the temperature levels are not right therefore creating blotches, and leaving old skin behind. Learn more in this chapter.

The Shedding Cycle FAQs

The eyes of my Columbian Red – Tail are milky white, is this something I should worry about?

Nope because this is part of your boa's growth cycle which is scientifically known as Ecdysis or simply shedding. You can expect this shedding process to occur throughout your pet's lifetime. All snake species shed their epidermis which means that the outer skin will naturally come off and be replaced with a new one.

The milky color is a sign that your pet boa is in pre – shed stage; among snake hobbyists this stage is also known as opaque or in the "blue." The milky look is caused by secretions that start loosening the old shedded skin in preparation for the Ecdysis cycle. You may start to notice that the color of your entire pet will turn in a darker or

Chapter Seven: The Shedding Cycle

duller shade of color. You can expect this to last for more than a couple of days to a week before you can see your pet return to its normal color. After which, your snake will begin shedding its old skin.

The Ecdysis cycle is a very stressful period for your pet which is why it's very important that you DO NOT attempt to feed or handle your boa during this time. However, what you can do to ease this somewhat stressful process is to mist your Columbian boa with warm water.

How often will my Columbian boa shed?

This will highly depend on your pet's growth rate. Usually, young boa constrictors will shed at least once a month while adult or matured boas may shed only 3 to 4 times a year.

It's also important to note that snake species undergo shedding period for various reasons aside from the fact that it's primarily due to growth rate. One of the reasons is stress. For instance, if you move your pet to a new enclosure or transfer them from the breeder to your house, the boa constrictor will most likely shed. Another reason is breeding.

Chapter Seven: The Shedding Cycle

Breeding causes unusually timed shedding periods. An example is when a female boa has just undergone the shedding process; if you place a male boa inside the same enclosure for breeding purposes, it will likely make her enter another shed cycle. Ovulation in female snake species also causes extended shedding period. The post – ovulation shed is usually a good sign for snake boa breeders.

What should I do if my Columbian boa shedded many pieces but some old skin remains on his/ her body?

Proper shedding means that the snake should shed in just one continuous piece of its skin. If that's not the case then that means there's a problem in the humidity or temperature levels inside your pet's enclosure. As mentioned in previous chapters, humidity should be kept at 50 to 60% all times. If you want to avoid this shedding problem, what you need to do is to mist your snake using a spray bottle. Make sure to prepare hot water in the misting bottle so that once it's misted it will just feel lukewarm to your boa. Every time your pet enters pre – shed cycle or once you see him/ her start to have that milky look, you can

Chapter Seven: The Shedding Cycle

mist your pet every day. Make sure to set the right humidity levels and spray all of the snake's whole body so that they can shed perfectly.

If you see that your pet has retained some of its old skin even after shedding, the best thing to do is to soak your pet in a tub of lukewarm water for at least one hour so that the remaining skin can naturally come off. You can also try using products like Shed – Aide/ Shed – Ease to help your snake with shedding problems. You can purchase it from your local pet store or online, and you just need to add this chemical to the lukewarm water and soak your pet in it. NEVER EVER peel off the old skin of your pet because it's not just painful, it's also very dangerous for you!

What is an eye cap and how is it related to my boa's shedding cycle?

Eye caps are the clear scales that cover the eyes of your pet. The eye caps should properly come off once your boa starts shedding. Make sure to check the shedded skin even if that means that you have to sort of unroll it to visually check the eye caps. If your boa failed to shed this area, the unshedded eye caps can definitely cause infections around your boa's eyes.

My boa seems to yawn a lot, is this related to shedding?

There are two possible reasons why your boa yawns quite a lot. The first one is because it's about to enter the shedding cycle. Your boa will need to yawn because it's a sign that it is preparing to stretch out its skin particularly on the head area. This is their way of loosening their skin so that they can eventually start shedding. The second reason is that if you see your pet yawn after eating its meal, this means that your pet is trying to re – align its jaw back into the normal place since their lower jaw usually stretches out whenever they eat a meal especially if it's quite larger than their mouths.

What can I do to prevent shedding problems?

Aside from the advice aforementioned, you have to understand that their environment inside the enclosure will greatly affect the humidity level. For instance, it's much harder to maintain humidity levels if the cage is an

Chapter Seven: The Shedding Cycle

aquarium/ glass – type of enclosures especially if comes with a screen top because the hot air will seep out of the cage. What you need to do is to make sure that you keep the humid air inside the cage. If you have a screen top, what you can do is to cut a piece of cardboard or any similar material, and just poke a few small holes in it; another option is to completely cover half of the screen top – these will help keep the enclosure humid and the ambient heat will stay there thereby raising humidity.

Another tip is to place one of the water bowls a bit closer to the basking zone heat source as this can also help raise humidity through the evaporation process of the water.

If you find that your pet has a hard time shedding off its eye caps, what you can do is to use a small scotch tape, and turn the eye caps inside – out. Make sure to carefully roll it across its eye area so that it will safely lift the unshedded eye cap.

Chapter Seven: The Shedding Cycle

Chapter Eight: Instant Solutions for Health Care Problems

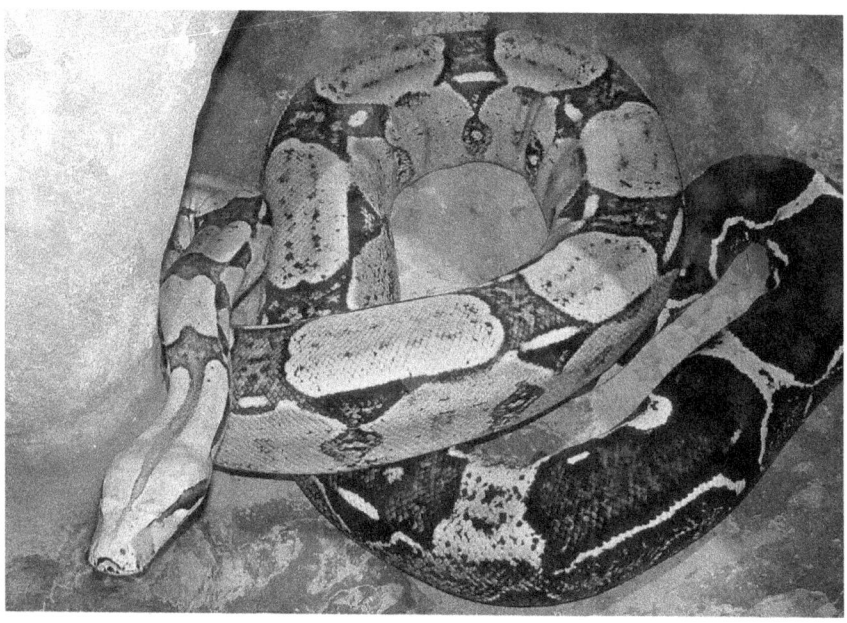

This chapter will tackle some of the most common health problems with boa constrictor species. You will learn what the possible causes of illnesses are, what the instant solutions you can do are, and what are the usual effects and symptoms of these common health issues. Improper husbandry practices are the main culprit in sick boas which is why it's best that you always keep their environment clean, well regulated, and a comfortable place where they are safe from various infections/ diseases.

Chapter Eight: Instant Solutions for Health Care Problems

Regurgitation Syndrome

If your pet keeps on regurgitating or sort of vomiting the prey item you fed him/ her, here are instant solutions to prevent it from happening in the future.

Instant Solution

The first thing to do once your boa regurgitates its food is to avoid feeding him/ her again at least for the next two weeks (around 12 to 15 days). The 2 weeks of no feeding provides a recovery time for your pet to rebuild the fluids that he/ she lost in his stomach due to regurgitation. If you feed less than 2 weeks, there's a huge chance that your pet will just regurgitate the food and make his/ her condition worse. Aside from that, it can also lead to regurgitation syndrome especially for young boa species. Here are the 2 causes of food regurgitation in snakes:

#1: Environmental Settings

Most often than not regurgitation syndrome occurs in young and juvenile boas because of overfeeding or improper

Chapter Eight: Instant Solutions for Health Care Problems

temperature levels. Boa species needs a heat range, also known as gradient, so that it can properly maintain food digestion. If the enclosure is always lower than the required 80 – 90 degrees F, then it will cause the food item to spoil which could upset their stomach plus the inadequate heat levels will create indigestion. If the primary environmental conditions are not regulated, you can expect your young Columbian boa to be susceptible to Regurgitation Syndrome. Pay attention to the environment conditions to prevent this syndrome.

#2: Health of Your Columbian boa

Considering that environmental issues are addressed, and temperature levels or heat gradients are observed, boa species that still continue to regurgitate may likely be due to another health issue like an infection or disease. It can be caused by internal parasites which is usually the primary cause of such illness. This will make regurgitation a mere symptom of the underlying problem. If not prevented, it could be life – threatening for your pet boa. So if you think you've done enough to fix the environmental conditions but

Chapter Eight: Instant Solutions for Health Care Problems

your pet continues to experience this syndrome, you better check for internal parasites and bring him/ her to the vet for further checkup.

#3: Fungal/ Bacterial growth

You may need to check the water you give to your pet because it could be the breeding place of bacteria or fungi. Make sure to replace the water bowls every day with fresh and clean water. Water bowls are usually where your boa will urinate/ defecate so if you don't replace it daily, the water will most likely become a breeding ground for these bacteria and can cause various health issues. Fortunately, fungal/ bacterial overgrowth can easily be treated by your vet.

After 2 weeks of no feeding, you can slowly start offering your boa with small – size prey items. It's also best to feed smaller food items over a couple of days to avoid this recurring problem. You may also want to change the source of your prey items because your supplier may be breeding rodents that aren't healthy or are fed differently. If you have already checked the environment, checked your pet's health,

Chapter Eight: Instant Solutions for Health Care Problems

and ensure a clean water every day but still your pet regurgitates then the problem is most likely on the prey item itself. If that's the case then the best thing to do is find another rodent supplier.

Lethargy

If you notice that your pet Columbian boa appears to be sick or feeling lethargic (ex: not eating, not active etc.) then it could be a sign of a serious health problem, and this should alarm you. Here are some instant solutions you can do once lethargy strikes:

Instant Solution

One of the first things you need to do is to raise the ambient temperature inside your pet's cage. You can raise it anywhere between 86 and 88 degrees. The right temperature level is perhaps the most important aspect of proper husbandry because it directly benefits your pet's health. Since they are tropical species you need to maintain the cage to tropical temperatures which is around 82 to 90 degrees;

Chapter Eight: Instant Solutions for Health Care Problems

the ambient temperature is around 82 degrees while the basking temperature must be more than 90 degrees. So if you think your snake is not feeling well, what you can do is to raise the ambient temperature level above 82 degrees. Your goal is to ensure that your pet does not feel cold especially when you hold them.

Raising ambient temperature levels up to 88 degrees can help out your lethargic Columbian boa recover more quickly. If you've already address the temperature level requirement and your boa still seem lethargic or perhaps loss its appetite, you must bring him/her to the vet immediately.

Respiratory Problems

If ever you hear your Columbian boa doing wheezing sounds or whistling as it breathes air out then there's a huge chance that your pet has a respiratory problem. Below are some of the solutions you can do:

Chapter Eight: Instant Solutions for Health Care Problems

Instant Solution

The quick fix is to raise the ambient temperature levels of the cage up to 88 degrees or more. You may also try lowering the humidity level to a few points as it could help in Respiratory Infection recovery. Make sure to consult your vet if you've noticed that your boa is doing the wheezing, whistling or popping sounds as it inhales/ exhales air. Your vet will prescribe antibiotic meds to combat such respiratory tract infections. Tylan has proven to be a very effective drug in combating respiratory problems especially in boa constrictors.

Respiratory problems just like in humans are caused by bacterial infection in the lungs. In snake species, it's mostly due to improper temperature/ humidity levels or inadequate environmental conditions. Some factors that causes respiratory infections include unsanitary enclosures, stress, lack of food, dirty water, and mistreatment among others.

The symptoms to watch out for aside from wheezing/ whistling are clicking sounds, audible noises during breathing, and open mouth (means they can't breathe

Chapter Eight: Instant Solutions for Health Care Problems

properly through their nostrils). You will also see mucous and bubbles forming around the mouth and the nostrils. You may also see that the head of your boa is slightly in a raised position because it will make their breathing easier.

Respiratory problems will cause your pet to be lethargic, lose weight, lose appetite, and bloated body.

Fecal/ Urine – Related Problems

If you notice that there had been changes in the feces or urine of your boa then make sure to take note of the instant solutions below:

Note #1: Your boa will defecate or urinate in an irregular schedule.

While baby boas urinate or defecate after every couple of meals, matured boa species may average once a month or maybe longer. Unlike other animals, snake species particularly boa constrictors don't eat and poop. This is because their digestive system has the capability to fully

Chapter Eight: Instant Solutions for Health Care Problems

utilize and maximize all the nutrients that they get from the food you feed them. Needless to say, the more infrequent they poop, the better because that means that their digestion is maxing out all the benefits it can get out of the food. Your boa species will have to eat a couple of meals before defecating. If you think your Columbian boa has already gone a long time without pooping, what you can do is to soak them in lukewarm water to help them defecate.

Note #2: Your boa loves to defecate and pass urates.

Your boa will defecate and urinate at different times. You can expect that they will produce black or brown stools. Their urates or snake pee are usually white or yellowish in color, it's also sort of a chalky substance. They usually deposit it on their water bowls which is why you need to replace their dishes with clean and fresh water every day to prevent bacteria/ fungal breeding.

Chapter Eight: Instant Solutions for Health Care Problems

Feeding Issues

If you find it hard to feed your pet Columbian boa with frozen or thawed prey items, it could start to become stress or even regurgitate especially if it's used to eating a pre – killed meal. Here are some things you can do to help your snake successfully convert into this kind of diet:

Instant Solution

The solution starts with you! You must do the 2 Ps when it comes to feeding snakes – Patience and Persistence. The most difficult part of course is convincing yourself but you have to understand that your pet boa will come along as long as you are patient and persistent with him/ her. Check out the tips below:

- If your Columbian red – tail is in good health, you can start offering him/ her with ONLY frozen or thawed prey items for a couple of weeks. Do it at different times during the day and at night. Keep in mind that

Chapter Eight: Instant Solutions for Health Care Problems

your Columbian boa will not starve to death if he/she refuse to eat the meal once in a while. So you should manage to have the strength of not giving in to feeding pre – killed diet when you see your slithery pet disinterested in what you're offering.

- Some keepers find success in offering different colors and sizes of frozen/thawed food. One of the biggest mistake newbie keepers do is that they fail to keep the rodents warm; place yourself in your pet's position, would you eat a frozen food? Of course not, you want it fresh or at least warm. It's very important that you just don't defrost the rodents, you have to soak it in very warm water for a couple of minutes prior to feeding it to your pet – this process is called thawing. The strong smell that's caused by heating their food will entice most snake species.

- Another trick that keepers do is to taunt the snake with the thawed food using long tongs. Once you're done warming up their meal, offer it in a slightly

Chapter Eight: Instant Solutions for Health Care Problems

taunting way to your pet, or wave the warm food around in the enclosure so that it can get attracted to the scent of the rodents. This method can immediately switch your pet into eating frozen/ thawed rodents.

- Some things you can do as what we mentioned in the feeding chapter is to use the hide box, to leave the prey item overnight, and to offer smaller prey items before following it up with a thawed rodent.

Important Note:

If your Columbian boa still refuse to eat frozen or thawed prey items after trying out different tricks, it's probably best to just stick with his/ her current diet (either pre – killed food or live prey feeding). You don't want to force your pet into eating something he/ she doesn't like because if it's prolonged, it could stress out your boa and can also endanger his/ her health.

Chapter Eight: Instant Solutions for Health Care Problems

Handling after Feeding

The question asked by most keepers after feeding is "how soon can I handle my Columbian red – tail after feeding him/ her?" "Do I really need to wait for 24 to 48 hours before normal handling as what others suggest?"

These questions are often asked because most keepers transfer their Columbian boa to a separate enclosure solely for feeding purposes. Of course, the separate feeding enclosure may not be adequate enough which is why you need to transfer the snake back to its original cage. On the other hand, some keepers choose to feed the boa in the same enclosure, and they're wondering when can they resume handling their pet boa.

So, why do we really need to wait before handling a snake after feeding them? This is because you want to give ample time for the snake to properly settle and digest their food. Otherwise they will definitely vomit out the food you give them especially if you're boa is still a baby or juvenile. It's like in humans, after eating a heavy meal; you would want to rest for a while before walking or going about in

Chapter Eight: Instant Solutions for Health Care Problems

your day. You won't certainly run, jump, dance or do any strenuous activity right after eating because since your stomach is full, you want the food to settle in the food and have it slightly digested so that you won't regurgitate. This is exactly the same with snakes; by handling them immediately after eating, you're risking them to vomit what they ate.

For Keepers Feeding In the Same Enclosure

All you need to do is to leave your Columbian boa alone for around 48 hours before you start handling them again. This applies for both young and adult boas.

For Keepers Feeding In a Separate Enclosure

What you need to do is to wait for 1 whole hour after your pet completely finish and swallowed the prey item. After one hour you can carefully pick up your Columbian boa and put it back into its permanent enclosure. Wait for 48 hours before handling him/ her again.

You see, you can temporarily touch or pick up your pet in order to place it back to their cage, there's nothing

Chapter Eight: Instant Solutions for Health Care Problems

wrong with that! Don't confuse handling with touching. Handling is when you hold your pet for a prolonged period.

Some keepers find that their snake is fine with handling even if it didn't reach 48 hours. You can possibly try to handle your snake after 24 hours. The 48 hour waiting period is just for insurance purposes.

Chapter Eight: Instant Solutions for Health Care Problems

Chapter Nine: Breeding Boas

The Columbian Boa is a very robust and appealing creature that can readily reproduce wonderful offspring in captivity provided of course if they live under the right conditions. This chapter will give you a background of what it's like to breed boa constrictors. Keep in mind though that the information you'll learn here are by no means the only method that these boas can be bred. If you think you might

Chapter Nine: Breeding Boas

be interested in breeding boas or perhaps you're just curious as to how these animals are reproduced and raised by breeders, then this chapter might delight you.

Pre – Conditioning

The most interesting thing about wild animals such as the Columbian boa constrictor, and pretty much all the snake species is that they will choose not to breed or lay eggs if they think that the existing conditions they are in will not make their offspring live a 'good life.' Isn't that interesting? Some animals even kill their own babies especially if they found out that the living conditions aren't adequate enough for their offspring. I know that sounds extreme but if you really think about it, these animals really care because they don't want their young to suffer the extreme conditions of life in the wild.

This is the reason why breeders of captive – bred boas make sure that they meet the pre – conditioning requirements of their pets just like in the wild. Otherwise

Chapter Nine: Breeding Boas

they wouldn't likely breed, or the females may choose not to lay eggs which could be a health threat to the species. Here are some of the pre – conditioning requirements:

- The male and female boa species must be compatible in size.

- The parents must have been pre – selected prior to mating to ensure that the offspring will also be healthy and in prime condition.

- You must cycle them up properly and consider the needs of both the species so that they can properly and happily copulate.

Sexual Maturity

As mentioned in previous chapters, some breeders breed their female boa constrictors as early as 18 months of age. This means that the female snake can give birth to their offspring at around 2 years old. Some breeders grow their

Chapter Nine: Breeding Boas

females to 5 ½ to 6 feet in this short amount of time. If you want to achieve this huge size in just a span of 2 years, you need to do a heavy feeding regimen. However, some breeders think that raising up female boas too quickly is unhealthy for them in the long term, this is why some don't follow this kind of method as it could have effect on the boa's health.

What some breeders prefer is to control their species' dietary intake and growth rate. For instance, you can raise both your male and female boas to just around 4 feet in 18 months instead of 6 feet as this is already good size for them to start breeding. Usually a 3 to 4 feet length male can successfully breed even if the females are around 6 to 9 feet. On the other hand, a 7 to 8 foot male boa may get stressful and even quite aggressive towards smaller sized females, and will most likely not copulate.

One of the indicators that your female boa is already ready for breeding is when you already see that she has a matured muscle mass. Most breeders agree that a 6 foot

Chapter Nine: Breeding Boas

female boa with matured muscle is best for breeding. A female boa of this size after par - nutrition can easily gain back all the necessary weight with regular feeding, and you can breed her again in the next breeding season. It's highly recommended that you maintain the 6 foot length for females because overtime it will produce more babies compared to much larger and longer female boas. At the same time, 6 foot length females will just need less food items and smaller enclosures compared to very large ones.

General Care and Husbandry

Male boas can be maintained in plastic rack systems or plastic/ custom – made enclosures (must be larger than their size). Female boas can be housed in 2' width x 4' length x 11" height. The enclosure set up is pretty much the same as how you would house your normal Columbian boa. The ambient temperature must be set at 82 degrees Fahrenheit, and there should also be thermostat, and a basking area. Natural light is preferred. The cage should preferably be on the ground floor to minimize vibration as this could stress

Chapter Nine: Breeding Boas

out your breeding boas. If you want to check them at night, use only a flashlight, and don't open a direct light on them. The environment where your breeding boas are placed should not have any other pets nearby, should not have loud music, and other pollutants like smoke. Always provide a clean and fresh water. Most breeders feed their boas every 2 to 3 weeks. The only time to handle your breeding snake is when it's absolutely necessary (transferring of cage etc.)

Chapter Ten: Columbian Boa Constrictor Care Sheet

Now that you've learned the basics about keeping a boa constrictor species, the next logical thing to do is to apply the knowledge and practical tips you've learned from this guide book. Keep in mind that the guidelines and tricks you have accumulated in this book are recommendations only, and that nothing is better than following your vet's advice when it comes to keeping your boa species. Have fun taking care of your Columbian Red – Tail boa!

Chapter Ten: Columbian Boa Constrictor Care Sheet

The Columbian Red – Tail Care Sheet

General Facts and Care Guidelines

- The red – tail constrictor grows to around 7 to 8 feet, and they can live for around 25 to 30 years in captivity.

- It's highly recommended that you buy a captive newborn Columbian boa instead of a juvenile or matured one so that you'll be the one to raise it and influence a docile temperament.

- Frequent handling especially at a young age will make them used to human touch; this in turn will make them docile their entire life and an even tempered pet snake.

- If a Columbian boa is in a pre – shed state, or you just fed them, they usually don't want to be handled – and if you do, they may display a defensive stance. If your boa seems to be aggressive or too defensive, you may need to adjust some things, perhaps their enclosure doesn't fit them, or the temperature is wrong. The

Chapter Ten: Columbian Boa Constrictor Care Sheet

aggressive behavior can also be caused by feeding problems, mistreatment, or illness.

- You should also purchase it from a responsible or certified boa breeder to ensure that the baby is healthy and of quality.

- When it comes to handling, make sure to always support their long bodies with both hands, and avoid making quick movements whenever you're approaching your pet otherwise he/ she will think that you're a predator.

- If you want to keep your pet boa docile throughout its entire life, you need to handle him/ her at least 2 – 3 times per week.

- If your pet wants to be left alone, he/she will usually create a hissing sound. Do not approach when your pet does a hissing sound because this is their way of signaling you to back off otherwise they will strike you. Your pet could be in a defensive position if it has health issues or if it's completely opaque.

- When it comes to housing 2 boa species, they can be kept together for a period of time within the day but

Chapter Ten: Columbian Boa Constrictor Care Sheet

they should still have their own cages especially during feeding times, shedding period, or if in case they get sick to prevent being attacked/ contagious. If you're planning to breed a male and female, that's perhaps the only times that you can house 2 boas together; some keepers can handle housing their 2 boas in one cage but if you're just a newbie keeper it's best to buy them separate cages because at the end of the day, they're still animals and you can't monitor them 24/7.

- Columbian red – tail boas can be quite messy whenever they urinate or poop. They usually don't defecate a lot but when they do; it's surely a chore to clean up. You may need to clean their cage at least once or twice a week as this is part of proper husbandry and of course to keep your pet clean.

Chapter Ten: Columbian Boa Constrictor Care Sheet

Housing Requirements

- **Custom Made Enclosures**

  Custom made enclosures are great for keeping proper humidity and temperature levels plus it's also easier to clean compared to aquarium/ terrarium glass cages.

- **Glass Enclosures**

  If you prefer this type of cage, make sure that you buy at least a 20 gallon tank size but if you can afford to purchase a much larger cage then it's much better so that you won't need to buy a larger one once your pet has outgrown the enclosure in just a few months' time.

- **Screen/ Top**

  Tightly secure it once you've set up everything including your snake because the last thing you want is for your pet boa to escape.

Chapter Ten: Columbian Boa Constrictor Care Sheet

- **Heater**

    You need to provide Under Tank Heaters (UTH) especially for glass enclosures. These heaters are usually attached to the bottom of the cage to provide your snake with their much needed warmth.

- **Ceramic Heat Emitter**

    This device can provide enough heat for basking and it can also be used as ambient heat. It usually costs around $20 to 25 and it can last for a long time.

- **Thermometer**

    Another important device is a thermometer. You'll need to buy 2 thermometers for your pet's cage. One is for the measurement of the basking area, and the other is for the ambient area. The thermometers should be installed inside the cage where you can easily see the temperature.

Chapter Ten: Columbian Boa Constrictor Care Sheet

- **Thermostat**

    You can buy various types of thermostat; some comes with dual devices, some has a nighttime drop feature that can automate cooling cycle and other features so it's up to your preference.

- **Water Dishes**

    There should be 2 water dishes placed inside the cage (if you have a large enclosure); the larger one should be on the ambient/ cooler area while the smaller dish should be in the basking area as this could help in humidity levels and also be used for drinking; having 2 bowls will also prevent your pet from compromising the level of heat required whenever they need water.

- **Substrate**

    There are various types of substrate that you can use including cypress shavings, aspen, coconut bark or even plain newspaper.

Chapter Ten: Columbian Boa Constrictor Care Sheet

- **Branches/ Hiding Spots**

   Providing them with hiding spots creates a sense of security for them especially if the enclosure is quite large. Boas rarely climb so most constrictors may not use branches that much. You can purchase grapevine or similar products for branches, and choose from various synthetic caves as hiding spots.

Housing Measurements

- **For Baby/ Juvenile Columbian boas**

   The minimum cage size for a young or juvenile Columbian red – tail is 20 gallon glass tank (if an aquarium – style tank is what you prefer); or a 2'X2'X1 size for custom made cages or plastic enclosures.

- **For Adult Columbian boas**

   The general rule is that the cage should be at least ¾ as long as the snake's body, and the width should be a third of your boa's length. A 6' x 2' x 2' cage size is perfect for your adult pet's lifetime.

Chapter Ten: Columbian Boa Constrictor Care Sheet

If ever you're planning in building custom made cages, just make sure to avoid unfinished porous/ wood surfaces as it'll be harder to clean and humidity/ water will definitely damage the material. The measurement is still the same 4' Wide x 2' Deep x 1' Tall to accommodate full – grown Columbian boas.

Husbandry Requirements

- **Spot - Cleaning**

   Most keepers use a solution of Chlorhexidine with water, just go to the store and find the product of your choice. You must first remove your pet and place it in another container so that you can properly spot – clean the cage. Wipe the entire enclosure with the Chlorhexidine solution at least once or twice a month.

- **Recommended Temperature Level**
   Columbian boa constrictors are tropical species that means that their environment inside the enclosure should be maintained within a range of around 80 to 92 degrees Fahrenheit as this is somewhat the

Chapter Ten: Columbian Boa Constrictor Care Sheet

temperature they have in the wild. You should also provide a basking area with temperature levels that's below 90 degrees.

- **Recommended Humidity Level**
You must maintain a humidity level of around 50 to 60% at all times. It's important to note that the humidity levels are actually determined by geography or your location.

- **Day and Night**
Columbian boas will need 12 hours of light and 12 hours of dark so an incandescent bulb may stress out your pet since it will provide a constant light just to heat up the enclosure.

If the location of your boa's enclosure is close to the window where it can get enough sunlight during the day then you may not need to buy any overhead light source like light bulbs, but if it's not near any windows, you may need to buy an incandescent bulb or florescent lamps for daytime display purposes.

Chapter Ten: Columbian Boa Constrictor Care Sheet

Feeding Guidelines

- The rule of thumb is to offer smaller prey items for your Columbian red – tail newborns; it's best that you feed them weaned or 'pinkie' mice/ rats before you gradually feed them larger prey items as your pet grows.

- Once your Columbian boa reaches its full – grown size, it's best that you start feeding them rabbits, jumbo rats etc.

Baby Columbian Red – Tail Boas (18 to 22 inches)

- They should be fed with fuzzy or pinkie mice/ rats. You can feed them 1 prey item at least every 4 to 5 days.

Juvenile Columbian Red – Tail Boas (2 to 3 feet)

- You can feed them 1 prey item once a week. You can start offering weaned rats.

Chapter Ten: Columbian Boa Constrictor Care Sheet

Yearling Columbian Red – Tail Boas (3 to 4 feet)

- They should be fed with small to medium size rats. You can feed your boa with 1 prey item or more (depending on the size of the rat/ desired growth rate) every 2 weeks to once a month.

Adult Columbian Red – Tail Boas (4 feet and up)

- They should be fed with large to jumbo sized rats. Adult female boa constrictors can be fed every 2 weeks while the male boas can be fed once a month. You can also feed your adult boa with rabbits, but the size of the rabbit will depend on the current size of your adult Columbian boa.

Shedding Tips

- Proper shedding means that the snake should shed in just one continuous piece of its skin. If that's not the case then that means there's a problem in the humidity or temperature levels inside your pet's enclosure.

Chapter Ten: Columbian Boa Constrictor Care Sheet

- If you want to avoid this shedding problem, what you need to do is to mist your snake using a spray bottle.

- Make sure to prepare hot water in the misting bottle so that once it's misted it will just feel lukewarm to your boa.

- Every time your pet enters pre – shed cycle or once you see him/ her start to have that milky look, you can mist your pet every day.

- If you see that your pet has retained some of its old skin even after shedding, the best thing to do is to soak your pet in a tub of lukewarm water for at least one hour so that the remaining skin can naturally come off.

- You can also try using products like Shed – Aide/ Shed – Ease to help your snake with shedding problems. You can purchase it from your local pet store or online, and you just need to add this chemical to the lukewarm water and soak your pet in it.

- Never ever peel off the old skin of your pet because it's not just painful, your pet boa can strike you.

Chapter Ten: Columbian Boa Constrictor Care Sheet

Health Problems and Quick Remedy

- **Regurgitation Syndrome**
  The first thing to do once your boa regurgitates its food is to avoid feeding him/her again at least for the next two weeks (around 12 to 15 days). The 2 weeks of no feeding provides a recovery time for your pet to rebuild the fluids that he/she lost in his stomach due to regurgitation.

- **Lethargy**
  One of the first things you need to do is to raise the ambient temperature inside your pet's cage. You can raise it anywhere between 86 and 88 degrees. The right temperature level is perhaps the most important aspect of proper husbandry because it directly benefits your pet's health.

  If you've already address the temperature level requirement and your boa still seem lethargic or perhaps loss its appetite, you must bring him/her to the vet immediately.

- **Respiratory Infections**

  The quick fix is to raise the ambient temperature levels of the cage up to 88 degrees or more. You may also try lowering the humidity level to a few points as it could help in Respiratory Infection recovery.

  Your vet will prescribe antibiotic meds to combat such respiratory tract infections.

Chapter Ten: Columbian Boa Constrictor Care Sheet

Glossary of Snake Terms

1.2.3. (Numbers with full stops) – The numbers are used to denote the number of a species, arranged according to sex, thus: male.female.unknown sex. In this case, one male, two females, and three of unknown sex.

Acclimation – Adjusting to a new environment or new conditions over a period of time.

Active range – The area of activity which can include hunting, seeking refuge, and finding a mate.

Ambient temperature – The overall temperature of the environment.

Amelanistic – Amel for short; without melanin, or without any black or brown coloration.

Anal Plate – A modified ventral scale that covers and protects the vent; sometimes a single plate, sometimes a divided plate.

Anerythristic – Anery for short; without any red coloration.

Aquatic – Lives in water.

Arboreal – Lives in trees.

Betadine – An antiseptic that can be used to clean wounds in reptiles.

Bilateral – Where stripes, spots or markings are present on both sides of an animal.

Biotic – The living components of an environment.

Brille – A transparent scale above the eyes of snakes that allows them to see but also serves to protect the eyes at the same time. Also called Spectacle, and Ocular Scale.

Brumation – The equivalent of mammalian hibernation among reptiles.

Cannibalistic – Where an animal feeds on others of its own kind.

Caudocephalic Waves – The ripple-like contractions that move from the rear to the front of a snake's body.

CB – Captive Bred, or bred in captivity.

CH – Captive Hatched.

Cloaca – also Vent; a half-moon shaped opening for digestive waste disposal and sexual organs.

Cloacal Gaping – Indication of sexual receptivity of the female.

Cloacal Gland – A gland at the base of the tail which emits foul smelling liquid as a defense mechanism; also called Anal Gland.

Clutch – A batch of eggs.

Constriction – The act of wrapping or coiling around a prey to subdue and kill it prior to eating.

Crepuscular – Active at twilight, usually from dusk to dawn.

Crypsis – Camouflage or concealing.

Diurnal – Active by day

Drop – To lay eggs or to bear live young.

Ectothermic – Cold-blooded. An animal that cannot regulate its own body temperature, but sources body heat from the surroundings.

Endemic – Indigenous to a specific region or area.

Estivation – Also Aestivation; a period of dormancy that usually occurs during the hot or dry seasons in order to escape the heat or to remain hydrated.

Faunarium (Faun) – A plastic enclosure with an air holed lid, usually used for small animals such as hatchling snakes, lizards, and insects.

FK – Fresh Killed; a term usually used when feeding a rodent that is recently killed, and therefore still warm, to a pet snake.

Flexarium – A reptile enclosure that is mostly made from mesh screening, for species that require plenty of ventilation.

Fossorial – A burrowing species.

Fuzzy – For rodent prey, one that has just reached the stage of development where fur is starting to grow.

F/T – Frozen/thawed; used to refer to food items that are frozen but thawed before feeding to your pet.

Gestation – The period of development of an embryo within a female.

Gravid – The equivalent of pregnant in reptiles.

Glottis – A tube-like structure that projects from the lower jaw of a snake to facilitate ingestion of large food items.

Gut-loading – Feeding insects within 24 hours to a prey before they are fed to your pet, so that they pass on the nutritional benefits.

Hatchling – A newly hatched, or baby, reptile.

Hemipenes – Dual sex organs; common among male snakes.

Hemipenis – A single protrusion of a paired sexual organ; one half is used during copulation.

Herps/Herpetiles – A collective name for reptile and amphibian species.

Herpetoculturist – A person who keeps and breeds reptiles in captivity.

Herpetologist – A person who studies ectothermic animals, sometimes also used for those who keeps reptiles.

Herpetology – The study of reptiles and amphibians.

Hide Box – A furnishing within a reptile cage that gives the animal a secure place to hide.

Hots – Venomous.

Husbandry – The daily care of a pet reptile.

Hygrometer – Used to measure humidity.

Impaction – A blockage in the digestive tract due to the swallowing of an object that cannot be digested or broken down.

Incubate – Maintaining eggs in conditions favorable for development and hatching.

Interstitial – The skin between scales.

Intromission – Also mating; when the male's hemipenis is inserted into the cloaca of the female.

Juvenile – Not yet adult; not of breedable age.

LTC – Long Term Captive; or one that has been in captivity for more than six months.

MBD – Metabolic Bone Disease; occurs when reptiles lack sufficient calcium in their diet.

Morph – Color pattern

Musking – Secretion of a foul smelling liquid from its vent as a defense mechanism.

Oviparous – Egg-bearing.

Ovoviviparous – Eggs are retained inside the female's body until they hatch.

Pinkie – Newborn rodent.

Pip – The act of a hatchling snake to cut its way out of the egg using a special egg tooth.

PK – Pre-killed; a term used when live rodents are not fed to a snake.

Popping – The process by which the sex is determined among hatchlings.

Probing – The process by which the sex is determined among adults.

Regurgitation – Also Regurge; occurs when a snake regurgitates or brings out a half-digested meal.

R.I. – Respiratory Infection; common condition among reptiles kept in poor conditions.

Serpentine Locomotion – The manner in which snakes move.

Sloughing – Shedding.

Sub-adult – Juvenile.

Substrate – The material lining the bottom of a reptile enclosure.

Stat – Short for Thermostat

Tag – Slang for a bite or being bitten

Terrarium – A reptile enclosure.

Thermo-regulation – The process by which cold-blooded animals regulate their body temperature by moving from hot to cold surroundings.

Vent – Cloaca

Vivarium – Glass-fronted enclosure

Viviparous – Gives birth to live young.

WC – Wild Caught.

Weaner – A sub-adult rodent.

WF – Wild Farmed; refers to the collection of a pregnant female whose eggs or young were hatched or born in captivity.

Yearling – A year old.

Zoonosis – A disease that can be passed from animal to man.

Photo Credits

Page 9 Photo by user Bernard DUPONT via Flickr.com, https://www.flickr.com/photos/berniedup/10364706584/

Page 14 Photo by user Bernard DUPONT via WikiMedia.com, https://commons.wikimedia.org/wiki/File:Columbian_Red_Tail_Boa_(Boa_constrictor_constrictor)_(10642424253).jpg

Page 24 Photo by user Caitlyn Capps via Flickr.com, https://www.flickr.com/photos/catsbrain/3732964877/

Page 37 Photo by user Caitlyn Capps via Flickr.com, https://www.flickr.com/photos/catsbrain/3732978757/

Page 50 Photo by user Caitlyn Capps via Flickr.com, https://www.flickr.com/photos/catsbrain/3733757380/

Page 60 Photo by user Lizzardo via Flickr.com,

https://www.flickr.com/photos/lizzardo/6827926514/Shedding Cycle Book

Page 79 Photo by user Maxine Power via Flickr.com,

https://www.flickr.com/photos/maxinepowerr/6955524901/

Page 87 Photo by user Dick Culbert via Flickr.com,

https://www.flickr.com/photos/92252798@N07/15622500991/

Page 102 Photo by user Glenn Bartolotti via Wikimedia Commons,

https://commons.wikimedia.org/wiki/File:Southern_Pine_Snake_eggs.jpg

Page 108 Photo by user Orin Zebest via Flickr.com, https://www.flickr.com/photos/orinrobertjohn/1501410683/

References

Colombian Boa Constrictor Care Sheet – ReptilesMagazine.com

http://www.reptilesmagazine.com/Care-Sheets/Snakes/Colombian-Boa-Constrictor/

Columbian Red-Tail Boa Constrictor – PetsForYou,com

http://www.petsforyou.com/boas.html

Common Facts on the Red Tailed Boa Constrictor – Mom.me

https://animals.mom.me/common-red-tailed-boa-constrictor-2910.html

Red-tailed Boa – Petco.com

https://www.petco.com/content/petco/PetcoStore/en_US/pet-services/resource-center/caresheets/red-tailed-boa.html

How to Choose Your First Pet Snake – PetHelpful.com

https://pethelpful.com/reptiles-amphibians/Choosing-Your-First-Pet-Snake

Red-Tail Boa – RightPet.com

https://rightpet.com/breed-species/reptiles/snakes/red-tail-boa

A Checklist on What You Need For a Columbian Red-Tail Boa – Mom.me

https://animals.mom.me/checklist-need-columbian-redtail-boa-10915.html

Boa Constrictor – PetMd.com

https://www.petmd.com/reptile/species/boa-contrictor

Boa Constrictor Care – ReptileRescue.com

http://reptilerescue.com/boa.shtml

Tips for Breeding Boa Constrictors – ReptilesMagazine.com

http://www.reptilesmagazine.com/Snakes/Breeding-Snakes/Boa-Breeders-Stone/

Boa Breeding Basics – SuperiorMorphs.com

https://superiormorphs.wordpress.com/2008/12/16/boa-breeding-basics/

The Ultimate Boa Constrictor Manual - MadAboutBoas.com

https://www.madaboutboas.com/app/download/.../TheUltimateCareManual-Published.pdf

Columbian Red Tail Boa Constrictor (Boa constrictor imperator) – BransonsWildWorld.com

http://bransonswildworld.com/columbian-red-tail-boa-constrictor/

www.ingramcontent.com/pod-product-compliance
Lightning Source LLC
Chambersburg PA
CBHW060837050426
42453CB00008B/724